MW01608197

Also by Robin Boyd
Among the Slow Roots

Field Without Fences

Robin Boyd

Dog Iron Press ⚬ 2019

Cover art: "Fences," by Stephanie Wells
Illustrations:
    Jean Mackay: "Flock in Snow"
                 "Along the Roadside"
    Liz Dvorak: "Feather"
Book design by Charred Pencil

Acknowledgements

Grateful acknowledgement is made to the editors of the following
publications in which these poems first appeared.

Agave — The Siberian Flamingo
Briar Cliff Review — Bird Blooms
Crab Creek Review — Cows Crossing
Cutthroat — Collective
Heron Tree — Depth of Field
                 Shaconage
                 What Matters
Northern New England Review — Three Poems About Three Horses
Red Eft Review — Time is a Dog; Space is a Cat
Redheaded Stepchild — My Father's Ashes
                 Fukushima Sutra
Slipstream — How to Speak Truth to Water
Whole Terrain — Floating Bog
                 Sheep and Light
                 Body of Earth
                 On the Sheepscot
                 Twelve Hours in Jemez

Field Without Fences

Table of Contents

For Kate

Ah, not to be cut off
not though the slightest partition
shut out from the laws of stars.
The inner — what is it?
If not intensified sky,
hurled through with birds and deep
with the winds of homecoming.

—Rainer Maria Rilke

Questions

Explain to me the intention of water,
how it traces the capillaries,
veins, then arteries of the earth,
racing downward,
always seeking its larger self.

Or the part of the salamander
that recalls its tail after
it separates from the body
and grows another, how the abstract
of memory translates to flesh.

Tell me more about the flight
of the monarch butterfly,
how it migrates from Maine to Mexico
on wings as thin as autumn ice.

Or how the length of day
will set a grouse drumming – spring or fall –
as it is moved to punctuate
the language of light
that binds the seasons.

Or why, two days before the summer Solstice
I find myself drawing deeper breaths
as if I could consume the utter density
of light before the slow descent
into fruition, seed and sleep.

Explain to me a hunger so divine
that one chooses
its unraveling emptiness,
the ever-leaning toward completion
as if desire were the answer itself.

The Mind/Body Problem

Golden Shovel from Han Shan, *Cold Mountain Poems IV*

You might say my
body is just the horse my mind's
riding into the
next sunset, gobsmacked by autumn
or love or the moon
rising or hope shining.

You could say my eyes – in
thrall to the rising tide and the
green-blue
flash of a breaking wave and the tide pool –
are merely reflecting
a memory of water glistening.

But let me make one thing clear
to my mind and yours – pure
and simply, there's
a way of being the body that has nothing
to do with the *I*.
Let me explain if I can:

It is the mind that will compare
your lips to a rosebud. It
is the mind that likens your hair to
a raven's wing. It is not what
the liver or the feet would say. What else
is there but that which the body can
insist upon – sleep and touch and the *I*
am of hunger – the body will always have its say.

Above the Arctic Circle

I imagine myself there in summer,
part of a constant rolling day where
the sun circles like a swallow
swooping high, then low, always aloft.

And how all of us – the people,
the plants, the birds and bears
would just keep moving with nothing
but hunger to mark the passage of time.

It would be an unworldly appetite,
a nagging deep down to consume,
to transform the plenty and cache,
as flesh, the abundance of light

for leaner, darker times.
I would save sleep for later,
after the brilliant pageant
of blooming and birthing subsides,

and the flesh stops moving
and the mind finally stills
to reflect on the madness
of bodies set loose by light.

I imagine then I could
surrender to winter like a child
swaddled, held close by darkness,
as day becomes the dream of the night.

Dark Energy

Science seeks truth by deduction.
The universe expands faster
than laws would predict, so there
must be something else. Something

invisible that swells like a storm
propelling us outward into the void
the way emptiness drives
the abandoned toward love, or how

one felled tree in an ancient grove will
send the others sprawling in its absence.
What presses most is the invisible.
It pokes and prods, reminds me

I am impelled by much that I don't know.
And, all the while, what can be seen keeps moving,
pushed (not pulled) by the expanding past,
the wordless flexing of the dark.

Einstein's Fiddle

His fiddle could conjure the breath of the breeze in treetops,
water moving downhill, rotating planets, the inspiration of moons.

For him, a Mozart concerto would lay down and relax,
uncoil its helix of sound, spin round in refrain

then break free to surge velocissimo through the narrows.
He was a man who would follow a melody upstream

against all currents to locate its source — the phonon
poised for first quiver, the Big Bang luminoso in C.

Rock # 84001

In 1984, a 1.9-kilogram rock believed to have originated on Mars was discovered in Antarctica and was later claimed to contain evidence of fossilized nano-bacteria.

Were there many rocks before this that belied the promise of heaven
that might have grabbed us sooner by the scruff of the neck

to shake our stubborn sights free? There have always been mavericks
who, with minds of their own, imagined such things—life

beating a rhythm so fresh it would never find a name among us.
Right now, right here, sulfur worms sway in ocean trenches,

grasses in a dark field, absorbing what is offered in abundance,
forgoing the popular comforts of sun and rain and air.

Fear demands a loyalty as hard as pure carbon, and so,
our affinity for molecules stacked in friendly combinations

like stone walls mark the boundaries of a field. We swear fealty
to the salt-laced liquids that animate our symmetrical flesh.

Right now, right here, a captive polar bear, when finally freed,
continues to pace, back and forth, the precise perimeters of its cage.

The Science of Finding One's Way

Consider the dampness that surrounds you
before you heed the direction of moss.

If you're on the water, listen before the fog rolls in.
Place the sound of the bell buoys in relation to shore.

Read the wind with your eyes closed and then open.
Note one detail in the distance and another closer

and then one more. Follow. Be aware of how weather
shapes the trees and where water wants to flow

to reach its end. Don't forget to look behind you
to see how the past appears from where you stand now.

You may want to return, or recognize you've already
been there, should you find yourself there again.

Time is a Dog

A dog marks time by smell. He knows
when you're due to arrive home as your scent
molecules dissipate with each passing hour.

He was waiting at the door ten minutes
before you turned left into the driveway —
his tail, a metronome, keeping time to gladness.

His wake-up call is an engine starting on a cold day.
It begins with a low rumble deep in the chest before roaring
to life as a full-throated bark demanding love & breakfast.

He is the grizzled muzzle as the years pass,
the lengthening naps, shorter walks,
long sighs of contentment by the fire.

He forces us to consider our finite lives the day
he politely declines his food. He is an interval,
a path to letting go and taking the risk to love.

Space is a Cat

Cats are like birds — they inhabit a world
both vertical and horizontal and are less
beholden to gravity than most wingless beasts.

They take on the shape of whatever space
they occupy — a cardboard box, a flower pot,
the span of the dining room table. Sunshine.

They kindly allow us to share their domain,
not so much as you might move an inch
or two to make room for me on a bench,

but as a librarian might welcome us
into the stacks, a nod and a slight smile
to acknowledge the pact of amiable silence
as we each follow our own curiosities.

How to Speak Truth to Water

Follow the grassy track down to the footbridge,
the one with the wooden planks all rotted and soft.

Sit. Swing your legs like a loose-limbed child
and notice the riverbed, the scarred banks,

the exposed rocks softened by moss.
Then take a fist-sized stone and drop it.

Watch as water resists the sinking stone
as the sinking stone resists water.

Look over there and pay close attention to
the yellow leaf, stalled captive in the eddy.

Then note the birch leaning low over the current,
the exposed roots, its inevitable end.

See water for the clear beast it is, one long muscle
flexing a full-on samba last spring and now,

late summer, shuffling a final slow waltz,
before the band packs up for the season.

Now, tell the water your story, how you too follow
a route the land has chosen for you – how it begins

here at this stream and travels ever-widening rivers, flowing
east to marsh and sky, past the steep winter beach and home.

The Shipping Forecast

Finally it's the sound that matters
Rockall Fastnet Humber Sole
Lundy Shannon Bailey Tyne

Sailors' terror tamed to a soothing cadence
Northwest 6 to gale 8 backing
Southwest 9 to severe gale 10

The reader's voice, a hypnotic sway
Very rough or high showers then rain
good becoming moderate or poor

Banks Rocks Shoals Bays
Here the locals fish and sleep
leal to the sea rising and falling

New moon Full moon Spring tide Neap
Gusts beat back the breath then
haul it howling from the lungs

Squalls snap sails like gunshots
trees crawl sideways low to the ground
while her voice draws a perimeter of calm

She is the oracle of wind and tides
the veil between now and later
the dawn that burns fog to horizon

Cardinal Winds

The U.S. coastal Tuscarora tribe used the characteristics of wind to fill in the points between the cardinal directions.

Shriek of pine alone wind
Trees in the way of dawn wind
Delta of sand and drift wind
Hills like breaching whales wind

Clouds scudding forehead wind
Thirst cracking bones wind
Mud like empty skin wind
Scent of ash and rose wind

Water weeping girl wind
Apples drumming ground wind
Acorns rack the frost wind
Eyes claw the dark wind

Ferns curl like fists wind
Ice echoes water wind
Hunger hollows sleep wind
Hunger hollows sleep wind

Road to Jemez

The horizon lengthens
and lengthens,
a curved edge, always
in retreat. The gaze

fixes on the far away,
looks past thistle and
pepper grass to the
gray rumor of mountains.

Distance is constant.
Distance is near.
The awake mind knows it
as sleep knows dreams.

Distance is what you
cannot see. What you
cannot see is what
distance compels you to

consider, to construct,
because in the distance
is time and space still
unwoven. A flash flood

forms in stacking clouds
to the west. Dust swirls
in the rising wake
of a running horse.

A seed lies dormant
in the arid soil.
The rain comes
and changes everything.

Twelve Hours in Jemez

The rind of moonlight illuminates the west canyon.

Passing clouds soften and ripple lit stone.

Pale light pulls one cottonwood from the shadows.

In darkness, cooling rocks draw slow, shallow breaths.

The desert is tidal, in thrall to what repeats.

Water finds root, fire licks seed, frost stings leaf.

Drought frees the untwined dust.

Sudden water heaves stone.

Asters shock the monochrome ditches.

Morning travels down canyon walls as if sunrise were a falling action.

Cottonwoods crown the riverbanks then follow the drift of light.

Dawn turns to heat and shoves wind through the valley.

Just passing through, this is what I know.

Mapping the Desert

The light was sculptural that morning
while others slept. It haunted the rocks and sand.

It animated the slow life of the hardened ground
and its uneven narratives of flood and wind.

I didn't follow a path but skirted the boulders
in a watery course that could have continued

until the land fell away to ocean. I understood then
how to be lost in the desert. How to be caught

by light and the details of distance. Each curve like
the next, each rock pile luminous with age and silence.

Waiting for Rain at the Salton Sea

Virga—Streaks of rain appearing to hang under a cloud and evaporating before reaching the ground.

I saw the virga. I watched it soak one small patch of sky,
a thumbprint riding low on the clear horizon.

On the ground I waited to be washed, to drink, my lips
parched and cracked as the salt-baked shores around me.

But is the nature of the virga to disappoint, its bloat of cargo visible
and useless, a promise broken by heat rising to take the rain.

It's like an old sadness that pushes behind the eyes,
pulses high in the throat and never breaks through.

That's the virga. I wish I hadn't seen it, had never
been reminded that water falls from the sky and flows.

I'd rather find a way to love this abandoned boneyard,
the pentagonal tiles that pave the shore like a palace floor,

the way shell is churned into the finest dust, dry and loosened,
the way it rises and circles in thrall to sere winds.

Kyrielle: *Exhalations*

The cat reels in his stalking breath
curled by my head as night reins day,
his rumbling sleep, the rise and fall
of breath anchor our dreamlessness.

Canyons yawn their saddened colors.
Tail feathers mutely whip the sky.
Water cuts stone like the gravel
of wind unravels flown prayers.

Wakened sighs are siphoned upward
to the night mills of exhaling trees
released to rush through canyons
of tunneled breath. Spun rock slots

sift the ragged remains of zephyrs,
cousins of wind tamed, buoyant
and neutral, as sun-warmed rocks cool.
Breath sinks, visible, hovering.

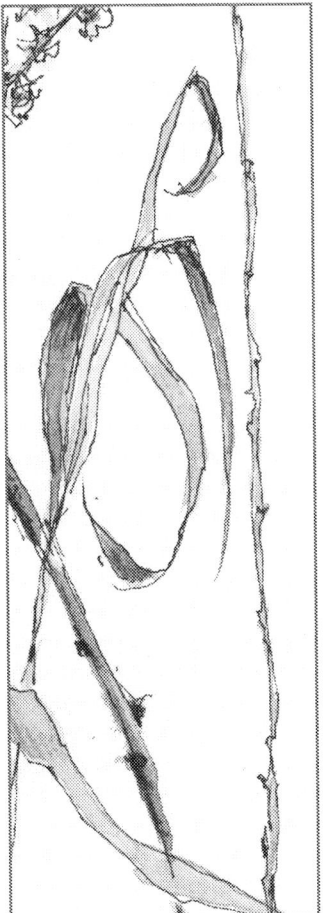

II

Body of Earth

I didn't reply when you said you may
not see another winter. Your words

just shimmered in the air as we
listened to the rain beat down.

I imagined your neurons, veins and arteries
as splayed networks of water and roots

carving themselves again and again
into earthly matter — both flesh and rock.

Like rivers and monsoons, we arise from nothing,
rage in the full volume of youth, then grow thin.

In the end, we are deltas, fragile and potent
with all we bring with us into the shallow bays.

At the Radiation Suite

Down here on L2, below
the well-appointed lobby,
below the parking garage,
the chairs don't match.
The art is store-bought.
Matting on one print lifts
and bubbles. On another
the glass is missing.

In this exclusive club, every
member knows the drill:
grab a faded green gown,
change out, sit and wait
to be called — everyday,
five days a week,
holidays and weekends off.
Until the tumor shrinks or not.

In this, our lead-lined suite,
we don't know each other's
names, but we know each
other's cancers, when they
were discovered, how long
each has simmered in the jaw,
the breast, the pancreas,
blood and bone.

We don't know what's next.
No one does. But we can't
pretend the unknown waits
like a latent virus in some
faraway cave. It's now, like
an itch or hunger or next breath.
It is a danger that makes us
friendly, desperately friendly.

And so, we wait and we talk
softly among ourselves,
compare side effects, appetites,
mood swings and fatigue.
Together, we are natives
of a small country, quietly
waging war against extremist cells
massing at the border.

To Name the Unknown

A jet lifts off the tarmac
and enters a world of invisible
currents, skyplaces called *MOTWN* and
NIMOY named after the solid ground below.

Geese lift off the ragged fields,
bellies full of corn and gizzards of gravel,
they name the ground *next*
as they trace the magnetic earth.

Above me the sky flows and shifts
in an endless blue silence that rejects
all names beyond *always* and *azure*.
And still the urge to pin a thing down

is strong when it cannot be held.
To give the unknown a name
and a place in the world – to say
I've been here before – renders odd comfort.

So, today, for you, wordless as you sleep
long hours in your hospice bed,
I will name the unexplored after
of death *a field without fences,*
and loss, *a feather swept up in the wind.*

Call and Response

At her bedside, I listened to her die,
short, then lengthening pauses –
a toiling routine.

Ladle of breath spills through
browning leaves. Trees beat back
the silence.

Every breath pulled from a well.
Every exhalation, a dusty book
slammed shut.

What's left after the burrowed air
is released but the impulse
to try again?

I've seen wind's parting language
unscroll across water's
thin skin.

Cloud banks contain swift currents
of sky. Dark presses down the last sighs
of light.

The pause grew long and became that.
I wanted to stay, to become
such stillness.

Ashes

The ashes of the dead
have surprising heft.
One expects light flakes of burned

paper beneath a cold grate.
But what we get has substance,
bits of bone suspended like grains

in a fine flour. I've held them,
run them through my fingers.
Toss them and the wind winnows

the gravel of bones from
the whisper of everything else.
Bone drops, obedient to gravity,

the dead weight of the dead
sifted from wonder's lift, while
ashes play on invisible wind,

its arcs and swoops revealed
like a musical score describes
a dirge, an arioso.

Pantoum for My Dead

Some slap in the breeze, ragged flags, barely there.
Others let loose like monsoons, sudden and drenching
or radiate warmth like sun against skin.
Some cycle around like comets and sunspots.

My dead loom like monsoons, sudden and drenching
or stand silent and empty like a field with one tree.
Some cycle around like comets and sunspots.
Others migrate like birds, nesting just for the season.

Silent and empty as a field with one tree
they come back again in dreams, again,
chasing one season, migrating like birds.
A dull ache, a rumor, a worrisome mole, they nag me.

They come back again in dreams, again
entering like film stars, even bigger in death.
Dull aches and rumors, a worrisome mole, they complain.
They spin, they drop, they ask for my love.

They enter like film stars, even bigger in death.
They float in on tides and trip me like tree roots.
They spin, they drop, they ask for forgiveness.
However they come, they are my own haunting.

They float in on tides and rise up like tree roots.
I live with them as I do every next moment.
However they come, they are my own haunting.
Revealed one at a time, unknown until now.

I live with my dead as I do every next moment,
hoping for warmth, for kind sun against skin.
Revealed one at a time, unknown until now,
they flap in the wind, pale flags, barely there.

Reflection at 4 A.M.

The body

breathes itself

as night passes

a black cat

watching the air

hurl a dark bird

toward dawn

casting shadows

as if in conversation

with itself and

then this mind

thinking itself

apart but not.

Fukushima Sutra

Gaki, a Japanese word meaning hungry ghosts

We don't like to cry here in the towns
over the hills from Fukushima.

We didn't lose anyone and the cracked
window panes all have been replaced.

But there is still much work to do.
The ghosts continue to crest the hill,

settle in our valley like a cold fog, appearing
sometimes sodden and always sad

in cabs, tea shops, gazing up from the puddles.
It is the nature of gaki to never be sated,

their deaths so full of questions. We dine with them,
listen, digest the void of unfinished lives so

the dead become us. We tell them you are here,
you are not here. You hunger and you do not.

The sutra says there is no suffering, nor end
to suffering. Stay, go. The water rises, retreats.

After the Rapture

Coyotes adapted, yet again, to thrive without traps and poison.

And prey still fled and sometimes froze according to its best instincts.

The redwoods and prairies took it all back — the barn, the tractor, the queen-sized bed.

Route 1 became a game trail.

The Suez Canal filled with sand.

Sky pressed down on the spreading edges of savanna of tundra of taiga.

It took one generation for each species to forget.

Then beasts moved together as one impulse toward water.

Migrations continued unbroken by fences.

Wind collected the catkins of birches, sowing them as it would.

Sulphur worms swayed in the ocean vents.

Whales sang a new language.

The boldest came first to reclaim their place.

The hunger and desire that drive life forward was never again described.

Nothing was ever measured again.

Unworshipped, the moon waxed and waned, moving waters
back and forth.

The only gods were fire and flood — the powers life knows how to flee.

The Self before Sleep

Despite the sodden world
weighed down from days of rain,
the darkened ground, sky low

against the trees, thrushes
ring bell-like in the forest,
and peepers saw the damp air.

I stand outside
and ponder the *I am,*
the constant mantra of self

who gathers in gratitude
the heft of this evening air,
the lightness of sound.

Who says, *I am?*
Who says, *I hold this?*
Can the bells be parsed from the rain?

Revolution

The moon is never full, you argued. It is
always turning; there is no single moment.

A stoat moults its pale winter coat from nose to tail in March
then reclaims it tail-first come fall.

Coming and going sieve one into the other.
Stars are cold before their light ever arrives.

By choosing we create the world

The cat muses at the window.
I know this because he is still,

at rest, in the mind that twitches
its tail as it waits for the bird.

The cat turns and looks at me.
He no longer muses. I know this

because he jumps from the table to
the couch and settles beside me.

He has chosen, rather than dwell
in the uncertainty of neither

where all possibilities still exist.
I watch myself consider this, then listen.

Have the thrushes sung like this all morning?

Sensation

Sadness dwells behind the ribs like a lonely dog under a porch.

And fear is a shower of ice from a hemlock shaken by wind.

The boy's mother leaving him without so much as a look back —

This is something else altogether because he is still waiting

And waiting, like wishing, cannot be pinned down.

And the term heartache became literal.

So the last white rhino is a thunderhead stacked high in my chest.

And hunger is waiting for the August moon to clear the tallest pines.

And love, when it arrives, takes me down by the back of the knees.

It's the one thing I have never seen coming.

Against Leaving

for a friend contemplating suicide

Why not the beech forest rising
gray-muscled against the snow?
Why not their papery leaves
rasping golden against a colorless sky?

Why not the tall window that
overlooks the orchard, now backlit
against a low December sun?
And the ferns green & stubborn

against the freeze, hemlocks
where the deer sleep? Why not
the small fires we burn
against the creeping dark?

We know the orchard will explode
the palest pink, bees will mob
the heavy blossoms. Why not this?
There are so few promises.

Love Poem in Heat Wave

Hot days are coming but today
we have storms and the wettest greens.
A hundred shades collide, a stadium crowd
of leaves and grasses, high and low,
all churn in applause for the rain.

The heat is coming, haze blurs the miles.
The water is flat, not a breeze
for ten towns. We sit on the porch
with sleeping dogs and beg the air to stir,
just grateful for nothing to do.

The heat is here my love, ninety degrees
and thick with sweat. We awaken
under thin, wet sheets. Your touch
burns and slides. I don't move away.
We laugh and wait for dusk.

Lamentation

Crickets and cicadas set the pulse of the evening.
It's late in the summer and the long light is precious.

The geese migrate, their calls lonesome,
lingering, sounding every possibility not chosen.

They loosen the roots of a life long held in place
by lilacs, peach trees, the beloved other.

We talk of leaving too someday when winters nest in our joints
and we're too weak to beat back the encroaching forest.

Tonight, two barred owls call and respond over and over.
And I can feel the life of the aging season slip into

autumn's gold pockets. In the air, I trace the shape of sound
with my finger and follow its progress past me, and gone.

Morning - Chatham, Massachusetts

Briefly, the air is silent. Early sunlight fractures
into panes and grids the floor. Next door a man rips
shingles from the roof. They drop with a loud slap.

In the kitchen, the grandfather plays hide and seek
with the beautiful boy who shrieks with a spark
of fright and the fire of more, always more.

The current of this last day together pushes on
and will carry us with it despite our wish to remain
loosely moored in morning's bright shoals.

I think of boats in the harbor and tin rhythms of metal
on mast and how affinities of sand, sea, dune grass
and sky blend together like a practiced choir.

Low voices on the back deck rise and fall
and, muted by walls and distance, become
a melody that inexplicably saddens.

From this Chair

I sit night after night after
work is done, the cats

and dogs, sated and quiet.
I watch the birds at the feeder,

grosbeaks and finches mostly,
an occasional pair of cardinals.

Hummers dash and hover
over the petunias.

The dull ache of a jet
groans softly in the east.

An orange lily, just for today,
dominates the green horizon.

When all color drains to darkness
I get up and move inside.

Nothing stays the same, ever.
Dusk captures the lawn.

III

Bird Blooms

In the evening when migrating birds rise
into the gray air to find the next marsh, cornfield,
or open water bay, they show up on the weather radar
as expanding spirals of pure loft like a flower opening
or Cabernet spilling on white cloth.

I think of all the things that blossom this way –
galaxies, a blushing cheek, music rising to crescendo,
how the first bite of tomato still warm from the sun
spreads on and beyond the tongue the way good news
and bad ripple outward from the epicenter of moment.

I have had the experience, but not for many years,
of seeing the boy I secretly adore turn a corner and walk
toward me and feel love unfurl in my chest like a bloom
of geese hurling themselves skyward for a long night flight,
one after another, all calling at once for the pure joy of it.

The Siberian Flamingo

after a story from Travels in Siberia by Ian Frasier

Some years ago, a flamingo fell from the sky onto
the shore of a Siberian lake where some boys

were fishing. It was November and snowing.
They brought the bird home, thawed its frostbitten feet,

fed it fish and it began to recover. Now, nearby,
there just happened to be an arboretum, really,

almost as rare as a flamingo in those parts.
They brought the bird there, and people came

from all around to see it. It was a holy tropical
visitation to the people who lived there.

The flamingo settled in as if it had planned the trip
and booked the room. The people named it Phili.

Flamingos take on the color of the food they eat and
Phili turned gray as the northern sky and the endless

steppes in winter. What, you ask, are the chances of a pink
tropical bird the size of a sturgeon falling out of the sky

to the shores of Lake Baikal in November within easy
driving distance of an indoor tropical garden?

I'm telling you this to remind you that anything
can happen. And it does. Because listen,

a couple of years later in November a second flamingo
fell out of the sky. Again, the bird was found by boys

and nursed back to health. This bird, named Phima,
now lives happily with Phili and they spend their days

together, dressed in Siberian-gray plumage, populating
a winter garden, two rare lights in the northern darkness.

Depth of Field

Two hummingbirds rise like small balloons caught in an updraft.
I'm not even sure I saw them, so quick and faint against
the foliage and so far away.

Goldfinches, still bright in August, claim the foreground,
hungry and fidgety, they push each other
away from the seed.

At noon clouds move slowly far and above, cumulus and cirrus
share one field, two fabrics, burlap and silk, pass one
in front of the other and never merge.

An airplane groans in the distance. It recalls Sundays from long ago
when the world was shades of gray and the rise and fall
rhythms of my father snoring in his chair.

Hours pass and the sound of crickets is a hay field grown around me
and trees are silhouettes against a universe made visible by night.
Far from here an airplane yawns the sky.

Collective

How many crows does it take to produce a murder
or larks to explode in a glorious exaltation?

Starlings murmurrate, dogs merge to packs, cranes collect
in a sedge, their necks curved like swamp grasses.

A simple plural won't fly when whales form a pod
or ducks build a raft. But why does the weight of two wrens

conjure a herd when its nest is the mere size of a goose egg?
Three goldfinches make a charm and hippopotami a bloat.

Cats come in pounces, clutters, and clowders.
For me, nothing stifles like a scowl of librarians

or tsks like a starch of nurses. A push of midwives delivers
a chuckle of babies to a maybe of parents and a repetition

of drunks loves to brag of the day when they belonged
to an annoyance of millionaires. Myself, I hail from

a complaint of Irish immigrants on one side and a halo
of Brits on the other. My great grandfather married

into a tribe of Penobscots and my great aunt joined an elite
brave of Maine Guides. Tonight, I will rest on a pleasure

of pillows as I gaze at a memory of stars that pricks through
the darkness, one huge expanse that knows no other of its kind

because it is a lonely of emptiness, a vastness attached
to nothing else, but holding the multiples that cleave.

Five in Translation

I   Egret fishes in marsh grass

II   Moon, it's twin, reflected in shallows

III   Feather   Stone   Shell

IV   Horse stands in the rain

V   Hand opens

What Matters

It's the horse that grazes,
unaware, framed by
a long green pasture,
narrowing toward the flank
of the mountain that changes
color like water in light.

It's the horse alone
among the apple trees
gnarled by age and wind.
And evenings, the barn light
framed by the shapeless dark
where inside warm mash

waits, seasoned with apples.
It's the sonorous echo
of her chewing, soft
as footfalls on the
barn floor scoured
smooth by work and time.

It's these things real
and imagined as I pass her
twice a day,
in the paddock
or the pasture – framed
by mountain, by sky,

by all in the world
that goes wrong.
Her head dips
ground-ward
as she nuzzles
the dark earth.

Three Poems about Three Horses

1

I imagine my dead sister rides the dark one
bareback into the dense foliage and disappears.

And sometimes I dream I cling to the roan who jumped
the fence first and kept running. She was the one

who parted the mist so the pony would follow.
All three of them running at dawn

through the field outside my window. My sister
was alive then, asleep in the next room.

She rides the dark one now, has somehow become
part of this story I tell over and over again.

2

I'm wary of horses. I wasn't a girl who rode them after school
or drew them in the margins of notebooks.

I only know about horses what I knew that morning in childhood
when I saw them escaping through the meadow.

I didn't tell anyone I saw them, their secret freedom,
the exhilaration of space opening before them.

I didn't know until I saw them that beauty
is a thing that lives outside the observer.

Even if I hadn't been awake and watching dawn fill the field,
beauty would still have passed by on its way

somewhere else — until the farmer found them, three horses
grazing in the meadow above the orchard, then led them home.

3.

What are the chances that I would see them?
That a five-year old girl would awaken, climb

out of bed and go to the window. What are the
chances that the ground would be shrouded in fog

and three horses would gallop through the mist
right at that moment. And that the girl would

be changed forever. What are the chances that
we become who we are?

Sheep and Light

At the end of the driveway,
just at the turn to the road to work,
the sun is at once demanding and diffuse,
a brilliant soft liquid
covering everything, entering everything,
calling all things to invoke their own light

except the sheep that drift
above the firm earth, gliding deep
through shimmering grasses,
rounded backs silhouetted,
heads down, busy in the light, so of the light

they are unaware, seamlessly entwined
in morning and meadow. And I, outside,
looking in, for once so grateful
to be a thing apart, to know
this moment as different from the next

and from all others, and yet hoping
were you to stand behind me,
I would become one more
dark silhouette held in this
season of burnished mornings.

Illusion

It's where the deer bow their heads by the stream

Near the patch of grass that goes green first

Below the wolf pine that stands in the center of the field

Like the thumb of god holding the world in place

While all else drifts here and there

Amidst the aroma of thawed earth

Sifted by breeze through the high pine boughs

That rise and fall like tethered boats in the sky's blue ocean

Where crows scramble and vie for space in the unclaimed air

There is enough kindness here and room for us all

Cows Crossing

The farmer places the orange cones
in the center of the road,
threads two ropes across

to define a path for the cows
to safely cross the road
from pasture to barn.

The traffic stops.
The cows cross slowly
and one by one we join them

in the splendid turning
of a summer afternoon.
No rush to reach the barn,

or for us to arrive home.
It is all of a piece,
one endless green expanse,

this moment running
into the next, the path
leading from pasture to barn.

The farmer taps the hind quarters
of each cow as she passes, a reminder
to move ahead however slowly.

And us, idling, inside this pause
and the next, as we watch the cows
turning now toward the barn.

Here

Here, where the heat of the sun stirs the dust,
another day there was an ocean —Han Shan

Here

where the breeze

trains the eye to

papery blossoms

shivering in hot sun

a low oak branch

lifts in the wind

like an oar

from water

shadows pulse

dark then light - tides

comb the long grasses

Bees Bathe in Roses

Bees bathe in the shy pollen of roses
like dogs roll downhill in the fragrant grass.
We cover ourselves in the brazen bloom

of the year when the flesh of the peach blooms
the color of sun and the heart of the rose
where bees swim in gold above tall grasses

and the fullness of light lays down the grasses
with seed as hips swell beneath aging blooms
that called with wild color the bees to the roses

the bloom that falls, a rose to the grasses.

On the Sheepscot

Along our tidal river work and sleep and work
ebb and flow by charts calculated years in advance

 by folks smarter than us who know how
 to divine the future from a stack of history

that repeats based on the moon that moving target
a skeet thrown up and shattered piece by piece

 as the nights pass until it disappears only to become
 a pale coin in daylight we hardly notice but when we do

it's a matter of wonder of how lucky we are to
have a companion as sure as the moon that muscles

 the water back and forth day after day for every lifetime
 there ever was on this river now slack as a mill pond

until the next great wash begins coming and going
like bluefish and rockweed — we evolve — offspring of its diurnal sway

Floating Bog

Every year the channel slims
and the bottom rises.
Fallen trees stymie boats that,

last year, passed easily. But this
could be the final time we float through.
It's the way it goes: deep water to shallow

to swale to bog that won't hold
my weight, to wetland, maybe to lawn?
Mud splatters the gunwales as

I look for water snakes basking
They feel my approach and slip,
wet leather, into the shallows.

The bog grows outward, muck rising,
solid perch to pitcher plant,
sundew, sphagnum and sedge.

For twenty years I've watched
this pond become something like flesh,
water gone solid to make a new edge.

Heron, muskrat, beaver, blackbird,
each drawn to claim the fertile margins,
thriving amidst the richness of two worlds.

Swallows circle the larches.
The still surface reflects the mountain.
A mirage. A premonition.

Shaconage

(shah-con-ah-jey) or "place of the blue smoke,"
the Cherokee name for the Great Smokey Mountains

I could lose sight of myself
here in the damp air
that presses down
into the hollows

then rises in plumes
in the cool of the dawn –
a soft filter to loosen
the horizon and muffle

the shout of rock exposed.
The ground yields as in
sleep when thoughts
lose their edge, morphing,

melding with whatever
stirs nearby. I could give
myself up, enter the mist,
measure the odd

nearness of distance in
increments of fading color,
a constant unwinding.
Even a seer would accept

this bargain – foreshortened
visions for these rounded hills
folded with smoke
the unlikeliest blue.